How to Write a

GRADES 1-3

Editorial Development: Marilyn Evans
                       Jo Ellen Moore
                       Leslie Sorg
        Copy Editing: Cathy Harber
       Art Direction: Marcia Smith
        Cover Design: Liliana Potigian
         Illustration: Jo Larsen
                       Don Robison
    Design/Production: Arynne Elfenbein
                       Jia-Fang Eubanks

EMC 799

Evan-Moor®
Helping Children Learn

Visit
teaching-standards.com
to view a correlation
of this book.
This is a free service.

Correlated to State Standards

Congratulations on your purchase of some of the finest teaching materials in the world.

For information about other Evan-Moor products, call 1-800-777-4362, fax 1-800-777-4332, or visit our website, www.evan-moor.com. Entire contents © 2008 EVAN-MOOR CORP. 18 Lower Ragsdale Drive, Monterey, CA 93940-5746. Printed in USA.

CPSIA: Bang Printing, 600 West Technology Drive, Palmdale, CA 93551 [8/2017]

Contents

What's Inside 3

Teaching the Parts of a Story 4

Trait-Based Writing 6

Step-by-Step Writing Units 7

   Dogs 8

   A Bike Ride 13

   A Loose Tooth 18

   A Giant 23

Types of Stories 28

   Retell a Fairy Tale 29

   A Pattern Story 34

   A Circle Story 37

   A Sequence-and-Write Story 39

Story-Writing Centers 43

   Can Covers 46

   Who, Where, When, What Cards 50

   "Start with a Picture" Cards 66

   Story Prompts 71

   Story Parts 77

   Story Form: Who is the story about? 81

   Story Form: What happened? 82

   Story Form: How does the story end? 83

   Train Tales 84

What's Inside

Step-by-Step Writing Units

How to Write a Story presents three options for how to address a writing topic: a group story, a guided story, and an independent story. Directions for all three are provided so you can choose the option that is best for your students.

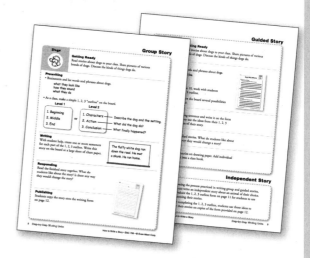

Types of Stories

This section provides instruction and forms for writing four types of stories: retelling a fairy tale, a pattern story, a circle story, and a sequence story.

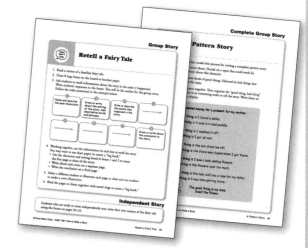

Story-Writing Centers

Questions, illustrations, prompts, and graphic organizers constitute five fun centers that motivate and encourage students to write creatively.

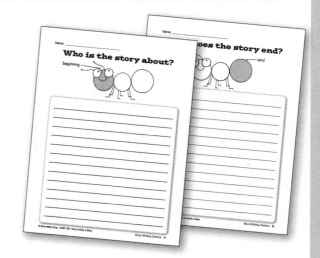

Teaching the Parts of a Story

Young writers often begin writing with no plot in mind. Learning to organize ideas to create a story with a sensible sequence takes time and practice.

Here are suggestions for teaching and crafting the parts of a story. Use Level 1 for beginning writers and Level 2 for more able writers.

Parts of a Story—Level 1 (for beginning writers)

- Explain that a story has a beginning, a middle, and an end. Each of these parts is important if a story is going to be interesting and make sense.

- Introduce students to these story parts by discussing favorite stories and deciding on the beginning, middle, and end of each.

- Then help students understand that a story doesn't have to be long to have these three parts.

- Draw three boxes on the board. Label the boxes "beginning," "middle," and "end." Read this short story to the class and help them identify the three parts:

Pete

I have a funny dog named Pete.
He dug a big hole in the dirt and got muddy.
I tried to give him a bath.
He ran away.
I tried to catch him, but I couldn't.
I called my dad.
He helped me catch Pete.
We gave Pete a bath together.

 Beginning

a funny dog

he dug a hole

he got muddy

 Middle

dog ran away

dog's owner couldn't catch him

owner called Dad

 End

Dad helped catch dog

they gave dog a bath

Parts of a Story—Level 2 (for more able writers)

More able writers may be ready to identify specific story parts—characters and settings, plot action, and conclusion. Use familiar stories with simple plots, such as fairy tales, to help students first learn to identify these parts.

One way to help students see the elements of a story is to create a story map. Draw the map on the board or butcher paper. Have students help you fill in the story map by identifying:

1. Characters and Setting—Who? Where? When?

2. Action—What happens? (the problems or events in the story)

3. Conclusion—How does it end?

Example:

① Characters and Setting

Goldilocks	in the woods
Papa Bear	in the bears' house
Mama Bear	
Baby Bear	

Goldilocks and the Three Bears

② Action

The porridge was hot.
The bears went for a walk.
Goldilocks went into the bears' house.
She ate food and broke a chair.
She went to sleep in Baby Bear's bed.
The bears came home.
The bears saw what she did.
They saw her in bed.

③ Conclusion

Goldilocks woke up and saw the bears.
Goldilocks ran away.
She never went there again.

Trait-Based Writing

How to Write a Story fits perfectly if you're using trait-based writing! When your students use this book, they develop these skills:

Ideas

- Choosing a strong idea
- Narrowing a topic
- Maintaining focus
- Elaborating on ideas and details
- Developing character, setting, and plot ideas

Voice

- Developing your own voice
- Examining different writing styles
- Writing from different points of view
- Using different voices for different purposes
- Choosing a voice to match your purpose

Word Choice

- Writing about action
- Using descriptive language
- Getting the reader's attention
- Choosing words for your audience

Organization

- Sequencing
- Developing a complete story
- Grouping together ideas and details
- Using different types of organization

Conventions

- Usage
- Spelling
- Grammar
- Mechanics

Sentence Fluency

- Writing a smooth paragraph
- Beginning sentences in different ways

Step-by-Step Writing Units

How to Write a Story provides three options for how to address a writing topic: group, guided, and independent stories. Choose which option is appropriate for your students, or progress from group to independent stories. If you have different skill levels in your classroom, *How to Write a Story* is perfect for you!

The step-by-step writing units on pages 9–28 guide students through the writing process at each level:

Group Stories

The whole class works with the teacher to create a story on a specific topic. After deciding on the characters, setting, action, and conclusion, the teacher writes the story on the board. Students copy and illustrate the story.

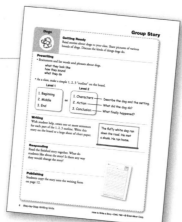

Guided Stories

The whole class works on the same topic, but each student writes part or all of the story independently.

Independent Stories

After narrowing a broad topic, each student writes his or her own story.

Dogs

Getting Ready
Read stories about dogs to your class. Share pictures of various breeds of dogs. Discuss the kinds of things dogs do.

Prewriting
• Brainstorm and list words and phrases about dogs.

> what they look like
> how they sound
> what they do

• As a class, make a simple 1, 2, 3 "outline" on the board.

Level 1		Level 2	
1. Beginning	**or**	1. Characters ——	Describe the dog and the setting.
2. Middle		2. Action ——	What did the dog do?
3. End		3. Conclusion ——	What finally happened?

Writing
With student help, create one or more sentences for each part of the 1, 2, 3 outline. Write this story on the board or a large sheet of chart paper.

> The fluffy white dog ran down the road. He met a skunk. He ran home.

Responding
Read the finished story together. What do students like about the story? Is there any way they would change the story?

Publishing
Students copy the story onto the writing form on page 12.

Dogs

Getting Ready

Read stories about dogs to your class. Share pictures of various breeds of dogs. Discuss the kinds of things dogs do.

Prewriting

- Brainstorm and list words and phrases about dogs.

  what they look like
  how they sound
  what they do

- Using the form on page 10, work with students to complete their 1, 2, 3 outline.

- Brainstorm and write on the board several possibilities for beginning sentences.

Writing

Students select a beginning sentence and write it on the form provided on page 12. They use the ideas from their 1, 2, 3 outline to develop the rest of their story.

Responding

Students share their finished stories. What do students like about each story? Is there any way they would change a story?

Publishing

Students illustrate their stories on drawing paper. Add individual covers, or bind all stories into a class book.

Independent Story

Following the process practiced in writing group and guided stories, students write an independent story about an animal of their choice. Reproduce the 1, 2, 3 outline form on page 11 for students to use in planning their stories.

After completing the 1, 2, 3 outline, students use those ideas to write their stories on copies of the form provided on page 12.

Name: _____

Our Dog Story

1 **Character and Setting**

What does the dog look like? Where is the dog?

_____

_____

_____

_____

2 **Action**

What is the dog doing? What is the dog's problem?

_____

_____

_____

_____

3 **Conclusion**

What happened last? How does it end?

_____

_____

_____

_____

Name: _____

My _____ Story
name of animal

1 Character and Setting

What does your animal look like? Where is your animal?

_____

_____

_____

_____

2 Action

What did your animal do? What is your animal's problem?

_____

_____

_____

_____

3 Conclusion

What happened last? How does it end?

_____

_____

_____

_____

Name: _____

_____
title

_____

_____

_____

_____

_____

_____

_____

_____

_____

_____

_____

_____

_____

_____

_____

_____

_____

How to Write a Story • EMC 799 • © Evan-Moor Corp.

A Bike Ride

Getting Ready

Read stories involving children riding their bikes to your class. Share pictures of kids on bicycles. Discuss the kinds of things that happen while bike riding.

Prewriting

• Brainstorm and list words and phrases about bikes.

what they look like
how they sound
what they do

• As a class, make a simple 1, 2, 3 "outline" on the board.

Level 1

1. Beginning
2. Middle
3. End

or

Level 2

1. Characters ———— Describe the bike owner and the setting.

2. Action ———— What happened when the owner rode his or her bike?

3. Conclusion ———— What finally happened?

Writing

With student help, create one or more sentences for each part of the 1, 2, 3 outline. Write this story on the board or a large sheet of chart paper.

> Sam rode his blue racing bike on a sunny day. Suddenly, he hit a rock in the road. His tire was flat. He had to push his bike home.

Responding

Read the finished story together. What do students like about the story? Is there any way they would change the story?

Publishing

Students copy the story onto the writing form on page 17.

A Bike Ride

Getting Ready

Read stories involving children riding their bikes to your class. Share pictures of kids on bicycles. Discuss the kinds of things that happen while bike riding.

Prewriting

• Brainstorm and list words and phrases about bikes.

what they look like
how they sound
what they do

• Using the form on the facing page, work with students to complete their 1, 2, 3 outline.

• Brainstorm and write on the board several possibilities for beginning sentences.

Writing

Students select a beginning sentence and write it on the form provided on page 17. They use the ideas from their 1, 2, 3 outline to develop the rest of their story.

Responding

Students share their finished stories. What do students like about each story? Is there any way they would change a story?

Publishing

Students illustrate their stories on drawing paper. Add individual covers, or bind all stories into a class book.

Independent Story

A _____ Ride

Following the process practiced in writing group and guided stories, students write an independent story about a ride of their choice. Reproduce the 1, 2, 3 outline form on page 16 for students to use in planning their stories.

After completing the 1, 2, 3 outline, students use those ideas to write their stories on copies of the form provided on page 17.

Name: _____

A Bike Ride

1 **Character and Setting**

What does the bike look like? Whose bike is it?
Where is the bike's owner?

_____

_____

_____

_____

2 **Action**

What happened on the bike ride? What was the owner's problem?

_____

_____

_____

_____

3 **Conclusion**

What happened last? How does it end?

_____

_____

_____

_____

Name: _____

A _____ Ride
kind of ride

1 Character and Setting

What did you ride? Where are you going?

_____

_____

_____

_____

2 Action

What happened on your ride? What was your problem?

_____

_____

_____

_____

3 Conclusion

What happened last? How does it end?

_____

_____

_____

_____

Name: _____

_____
title

_____

_____

_____

_____

_____

_____

_____

_____

_____

_____

_____

_____

_____

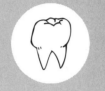

A Loose Tooth

Getting Ready
Read stories about loose teeth to your class. Discuss the kinds of things that happen in the stories.

Prewriting
• Brainstorm and list words and phrases about loose teeth.

> what a loose tooth looks like
> how kids sound with a loose tooth
> what could happen to the loose tooth

• As a class, make a simple 1, 2, 3 "outline" on the board.

Level 1

1. Beginning
2. Middle
3. End

or

Level 2

1. Characters — Describe the child and his or her loose tooth. Describe the setting.
2. Action — What happened to the loose tooth?
3. Conclusion — What finally happened?

Writing
With student help, create one or more sentences for each part of the 1, 2, 3 outline. Write this story on the board or a large sheet of chart paper.

> Susie bit into an apple at school. Ouch! She touched her front tooth. It was loose. She wiggled it all day. Finally, it fell out!

Responding
Read the finished story together. What do students like about the story? Is there any way they would change the story?

Publishing
Students copy the story onto the writing form on page 22.

A Loose Tooth

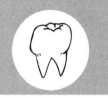

Getting Ready
Read stories about loose teeth to your class. Discuss the kinds of things that happen in the stories.

Prewriting
- Brainstorm and list words and phrases about loose teeth.

  what a loose tooth looks like
  how kids sound with a loose tooth
  what could happen to the loose tooth

- Using the form on page 20, work with students to complete their 1, 2, 3 outline.

- Brainstorm and write on the board several possibilities for beginning sentences.

Writing
Students select a beginning sentence and write it on the form provided on page 22. They use the ideas from their 1, 2, 3 outline to develop the rest of their story.

Responding
Students share their finished stories. What do students like about each story? Is there any way they would change a story?

Publishing
Students illustrate their stories on drawing paper. Add individual covers, or bind all stories into a class book.

Independent Story

Teeth

Following the process practiced in writing group and guided stories, students write an independent story about teeth. Reproduce the 1, 2, 3 outline form on page 21 for students to use in planning their stories.

After completing the 1, 2, 3 outline, students use those ideas to write their stories on copies of the form provided on page 22.

Name: ______________________________

Guided Story
1, 2, 3 Outline

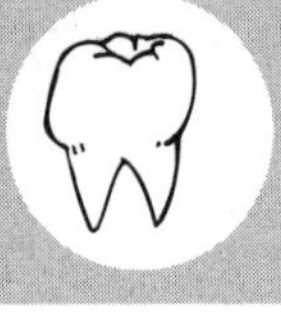

A Loose Tooth

1 Character and Setting

Whose tooth is it? Where does the story happen?

____

____

____

____

2 Action

What happened to the loose tooth? What was the problem?

____

____

____

____

3 Conclusion

What happened last? How does it end?

____

____

____

____

Name: _____

Teeth

1 Character and Setting

Whose teeth are they? Where does the story happen?

_____

_____

_____

_____

2 Action

What happened to the teeth? or How are the teeth used?

_____

_____

_____

_____

3 Conclusion

What happened last? How does it end?

_____

_____

_____

_____

Name: _____

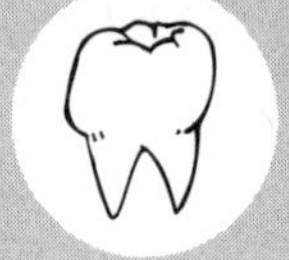

_____
title

_____

_____

_____

_____

_____

_____

_____

_____

_____

_____

_____

_____

_____

_____

A Giant

Getting Ready

Read stories about giants to your class. Discuss the kinds of things that happen in the stories.

Prewriting

• Brainstorm and list words and phrases about giants.

> what the giant looks like
> how the giant behaves
> what could happen to the giant

• As a class, make a simple 1, 2, 3 "outline" on the board.

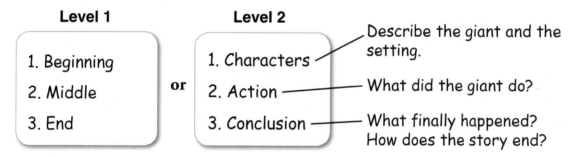

Level 1

1. Beginning
2. Middle
3. End

or

Level 2

1. Characters ——— Describe the giant and the setting.
2. Action ——— What did the giant do?
3. Conclusion ——— What finally happened? How does the story end?

Writing

With student help, create one or more sentences for each part of the 1, 2, 3 outline. Write this story on the board or a large sheet of chart paper.

> The friendly giant tromped through the forest. He came upon a big purple mushroom. It looked tasty! He took a bite. Zap! He was now a midget.

Responding

Read the finished story together. What do students like about the story? Is there any way they would change the story?

Publishing

Students copy the story onto the writing form on page 27.

A Giant

Getting Ready

Read stories about giants to your class. Discuss the kinds of things that happen in the stories.

Prewriting

• Brainstorm and list words and phrases about giants.

  what the giant looks like
  how the giant behaves
  what could happen to the giant

• Using the form on the facing page, work with students to complete their 1, 2, 3 outline.

• Brainstorm and write on the board several possibilities for beginning sentences.

Writing

Students select a beginning sentence and write it on the form provided on page 27. They use the ideas from their 1, 2, 3 outline to develop the rest of their story.

Responding

Students share their finished stories. What do students like about each story? Is there any way they would change a story?

Publishing

Students illustrate their stories on drawing paper. Add individual covers, or bind all stories into a class book.

An Imaginary Creature

Following the process practiced in writing group and guided stories, students write an independent story about an imaginary creature of their choice. Reproduce the 1, 2, 3 outline form on page 26 for students to use in planning their stories.

After completing the 1, 2, 3 outline, students use those ideas to write their stories on copies of the form provided on page 27.

Name: ______________________________

Guided Story
1, 2, 3 Outline

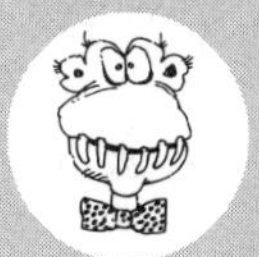

A Giant

1 Character and Setting

What does the giant look like? Where does the story happen?

____

____

____

____

2 Action

What did the giant do? or What happened to the giant?
What was the problem?

____

____

____

____

3 Conclusion

What happened last? How does it end?

____

____

____

____

Name: _____

A _____
name of the creature

1 Character and Setting

What does the creature look like? Where does the story happen?

_____

_____

_____

_____

2 Action

What did the creature do? or What happened to the creature?
What was the problem?

_____

_____

_____

_____

3 Conclusion

What happened last? How does it end?

_____

_____

_____

_____

Name: _____

_____
title

Types of Stories

Pages 29–42 provide experience in writing four different types of stories:

Retell a Fairy Tale
(pages 29–33)

Students use the familiar plot and format of a fairy tale to retell the tale in their own words. Instructions and forms are provided for group and independent stories.

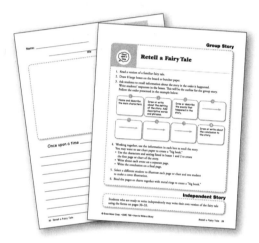

A Pattern Story
(pages 34–36)

Students follow a "good, bad, good" pattern to write a simple or a complete group story. In the simple group story, each student contributes a page. In the complete group story, the class writes one longer, cohesive story.

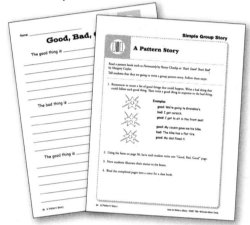

A Circle Story
(pages 37 and 38)

Circle stories require that each item leads to the next and that the story ends up where it started. Directions and a template are provided to write a group circle story.

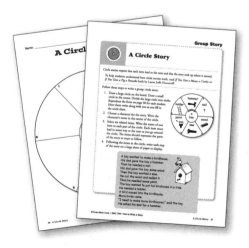

A Sequence-and-Write Story
(pages 39–42)

Students use pictures to illustrate the sequence of a story that will guide them to create a clear beginning, middle, and end. Directions are provided for group and independent stories.

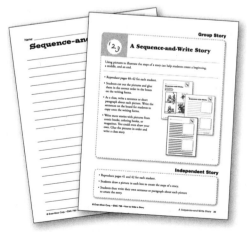

How to Write a Story • EMC 799 • © Evan-Moor Corp.

Retell a Fairy Tale

1. Read a version of a familiar fairy tale.

2. Draw 8 large boxes on the board or butcher paper.

3. Ask students to recall information about the story in the order it happened. Write students' responses in the boxes. This will be the outline for the group story. Follow the order presented in the example below:

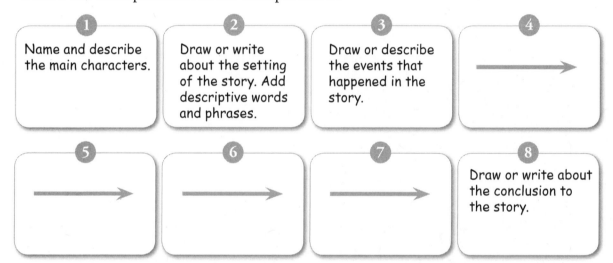

4. Working together, use the information in each box to retell the story. You may want to use chart paper to create a "big book."
   - Use the characters and setting listed in boxes 1 and 2 to create the first page or chart of the story.
   - Write about each event on a separate page.
   - Write the conclusion on a final page.

5. Select a different student to illustrate each page or chart and one student to make a cover illustration.

6. Bind the pages or charts together with metal rings to create a "big book."

Independent Story

Students who are ready to write independently may write their own version of the fairy tale using the forms on pages 30–33.

Name: ______________________

Once upon a time

____
title

Once upon a time ______________________

Name: _____

Once upon a time

First, _____

_____

_____

_____

_____

_____

_____

Next, _____

_____

_____

_____

_____

_____

_____

Name: _____

Then, _____

_____

_____

_____

_____

_____

_____

How to Write a Story • EMC 799 • © Evan-Moor Corp.

Name: _____

Once upon a time

At last, _____

_____

_____

_____

_____

_____

_____

_____

_____

_____

_____

_____

The End

A Pattern Story

Read a pattern book such as *Fortunately* by Remy Charlip or *That's Good! That's Bad!* by Margery Cuyler.

Tell students that they are going to write a group pattern story. Follow these steps:

1. Brainstorm to create a list of good things that could happen. Write a bad thing that could follow each good thing. Then write a good thing in response to the bad thing.

Examples

    good: We're going to Grandma's.

    bad: I get carsick.

    good: I get to sit in the front seat.

    good: My cousin gave me his bike.

    bad: The bike has a flat tire.

    good: My dad fixed it.

2. Using the form on page 36, have each student write one "Good, Bad, Good" page.

3. Have students illustrate their stories in the boxes.

4. Bind the completed pages into a cover for a class book.

A Pattern Story

For more advanced students, model this process for writing a complete pattern story:

- Think of a character to write about. Decide on a topic that could work for a "Good, Bad, Good" story about this character.

- Brainstorm to list different kinds of good things, followed by bad things that could happen related to the topic.

- Write an opening statement together. Then organize the "good thing, bad thing" items created by the class in an interesting order to tell the story. Write these on a large sheet of paper to display.

> **I needed money for a present for my mother.**
>
> The **good thing** is I found a dollar.
> The **bad thing** is it was in a mud puddle.
>
> The **good thing** is I washed it off.
> The **bad thing** is I got all wet.
>
> The **good thing** is the sun dried me off.
> The **bad thing** is the store was closed when I got there.
>
> The **good thing** is I saw a lady selling flowers.
> The **bad thing** is the flowers cost too much.
>
> The **good thing** is the lady sold me a rose for my dollar.
> The **bad thing** is I was late getting home.
>
> **The good thing is my mom loved the flower.**

Name: _____

Good, Bad, Good

The good thing is _____

_____

_____

_____

_____

_____

The bad thing is _____

_____

_____

_____

_____

_____

The good thing is _____

_____

_____

_____

_____

_____

A Circle Story

Circle stories require that each item leads to the next and that the story ends up where it started.

To help students understand how circle stories work, read *If You Give a Mouse a Cookie* or *If You Give a Pig a Pancake* both by Laura Joffe Numeroff.

Follow these steps to write a group circle story:

1. Draw a large circle on the board. Draw a small circle in the center. Divide the large circle into sixths. Reproduce the form on page 38 for each student. Have them write along with you as you fill in the circle chart.

2. Choose a character for the story. Write the character's name in the center of the circle.

3. Select six related items. Write the name of one item in each part of the circle. Each item must lead in some way to the next as you go around the circle. The items should represent the parts of the story or steps to follow.

4. Following the items in the circle, write each step of the story on a large sheet of paper to display.

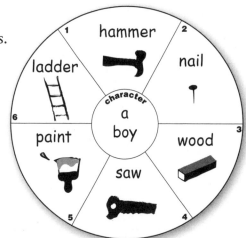

A boy wanted to make a birdhouse.
His dad gave the boy a hammer.
Then he needed a nail.
His dad gave the boy some wood.
Then the boy wanted a saw.
He cut the wood and nailed it.
Then he needed some paint.
The boy wanted to put his birdhouse in a tree.
He needed a ladder.
A bird moved into the birdhouse.
More birds came.
"I need to make more birdhouses," said the boy.
He asked his dad for a hammer.

Name: _____

A Circle Story

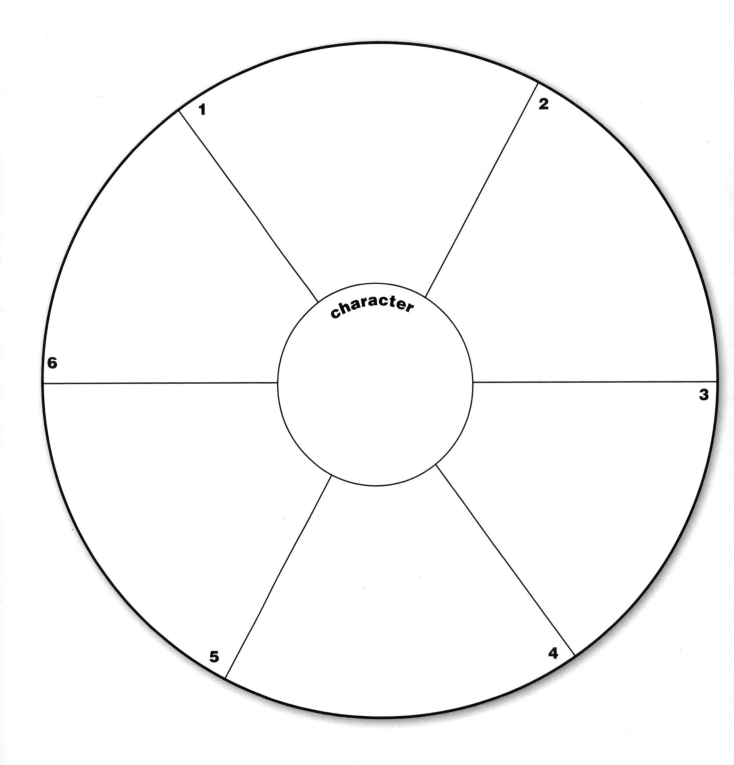

A Sequence-and-Write Story

Using pictures to illustrate the steps of a story can help students create a beginning, a middle, and an end.

• Reproduce pages 40–42 for each student.

• Students cut out the pictures and glue them in the correct order in the boxes on the writing forms.

• As a class, write a sentence or short paragraph about each picture. Write the sentences on the board for students to copy onto the writing forms.

• Write more stories with pictures from comic books, coloring books, or magazines. You could even draw your own. Glue the pictures in order and write a class story.

Independent Story

• Reproduce pages 41 and 42 for each student.

• Students draw a picture in each box to create the steps of a story.

• Students then write their own sentence or paragraph about each picture to create the story.

Sequence-and-Write

Cut on the dotted lines.
Glue the pictures in order.
Write about each picture.

Sequence-and-Write

123

_____

_____

_____

_____

_____

_____

_____

_____

_____

_____

_____

_____

_____

_____

_____

Name: _____

1
2
3

_____

_____

_____

_____

_____

_____

_____

_____

_____

_____

_____

_____

_____

_____

Story-Writing Centers

Once students are ready for independent story writing, set up a story-writing center! Materials for five centers are provided to keep students writing all year long. See pages 44 and 45 for directions.

Model each activity thoroughly before expecting your students to do them independently. Be sure to place different types of paper and writing implements at the center to help motivate your young authors.

Who, Where, When, What
(pages 46–65)

In this center, students use 4 Ws (Who, Where, When, and What) to create a story outline, adding their own details and conclusion.

Start with a Picture
(pages 66–70)

In this center, pictures initiate the writing. Students write a story about what is shown in the illustration.

Story Prompts
(pages 71–76)

In this center, students choose story prompts to complete.

Story Parts
(pages 77–83)

An ant stars in this center that focuses on helping students write a complete story with a beginning, middle, and end.

Train Tales
(pages 84–94)

This center helps students further develop the middle of their stories. Students use three train cars between an engine and a caboose to represent the plot action.

Who, Where, When, What

Materials
- four small cans
- colored construction paper 5" x 13" (13 x 33 cm)
- can covers on pages 46–49, reproduced
- *who, where, when, what* cards on pages 50–65, reproduced, mounted on poster board, and laminated

Steps to Follow
1. Cover each can with colored construction paper.
2. Glue the can covers to the cans.
3. Cut the cards apart and place them in the cans.
4. Set the cans at the center.
5. Students select one card from each can to form the outline of a story. They add their own details and conclusion.

Start with a Picture

Materials
- picture cards on pages 66–70, reproduced, mounted on poster board, and laminated
- storage box

Steps to Follow
1. Students select a picture card.
2. Students write a story about what is shown in the illustration.

Story Prompts

Materials
- Story prompts on pages 71–76, reproduced, mounted on poster board, and laminated
- storage box or can

Steps to Follow
1. Students select a story prompt.
2. Students write a story about the prompt.

Sam and Pam went to the park…

I saw a bunny in the garden. It was…

Story Parts

Materials

- ant forms on pages 77–80, colored and cut out
- ant writing forms on pages 81–83, reproduce multiple copies

Steps to Follow

1. Pin the ant forms to the center bulletin board.
2. Place writing forms on the center table.
3. Students use the forms to guide them in writing a story.

Train Tales

Materials

- train forms on pages 84–91, colored and cut apart
- train writing forms on pages 92–94, reproduce multiple copies

Steps to Follow

1. Glue together the parts of the engine, the cars, and the caboose. Pin the train pieces in order to the center bulletin board.
2. Place writing forms on the center table.
3. Students use the forms to guide them in writing a story.

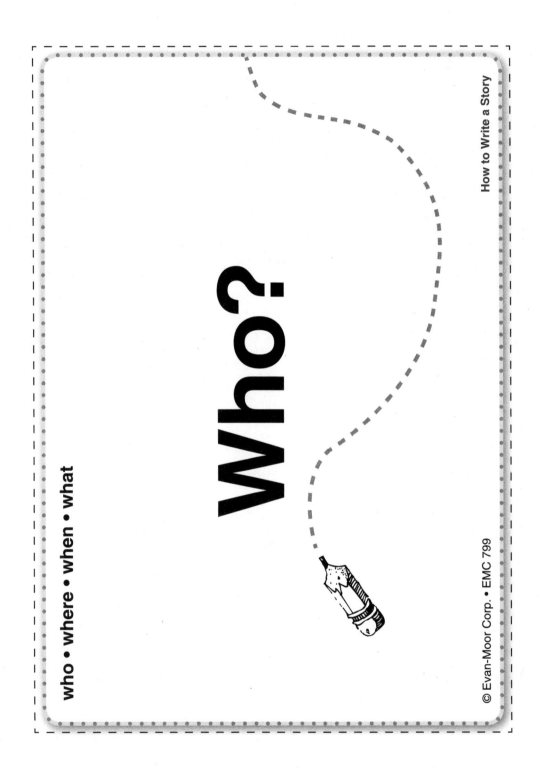

Who?

who • where • when • what

© Evan-Moor Corp. • EMC 799

who • where • when • what

Where?

who • where • when • what

When?

How to Write a Story

who • where • when • what

**Did
What?**

© Evan-Moor Corp. • EMC 799

Note: Use the cards on pages 50–65 with “Who, Where, When, What” on page 44.

who • where • when • what

big brown bear

How to Write a Story

© Evan-Moor Corp. • EMC 799

who • where • when • what

funny puppy

How to Write a Story

© Evan-Moor Corp. • EMC 799

who • where • when • what

noisy baby

How to Write a Story

© Evan-Moor Corp. • EMC 799

who • where • when • what

hungry lion

How to Write a Story

who • where • when • what

little boy with a wagon

How to Write a Story

who • where • when • what

a new bike

How to Write a Story

who • where • when • what

my pet pony

How to Write a Story

who • where • when • what

lazy girl

How to Write a Story

who • where • when • what

old man with a fishing pole

How to Write a Story

who • where • when • what

brave princess

who • where • when • what

tired cowboy

who • where • when • what

three little kittens

Card 1

who • where • when • what

dark night

Card 2

who • where • when • what

in the morning

Card 3

who • where • when • what

after school

who • where • when • what

last week

How to Write a Story

who • where • when • what

on my birthday

How to Write a Story

who • where • when • what

summertime

How to Write a Story

who • where • when • what

tomorrow

How to Write a Story

who • where • when • what

bedtime

How to Write a Story

who • where • when • what

one snowy day

How to Write a Story

who • where • when • what

when my work was done

How to Write a Story

who • where • when • what

after the game

How to Write a Story

who • where • when • what

next month

How to Write a Story

who • where • when • what

at the beach

who • where • when • what

under the table

who • where • when • what

in the backyard

who • where • when • what

downtown

How to Write a Story

who • where • when • what

at a birthday party

How to Write a Story

who • where • when • what

on the way to school

How to Write a Story

who • where • when • what

at Grandma's house

who • where • when • what

at the zoo

who • where • when • what

on a boat

who • where • when • what

in a treehouse

How to Write a Story

who • where • when • what

beside the river

How to Write a Story

who • where • when • what

next door

How to Write a Story

Card 1

who • where • when • what

fell into a hole

Card 2

who • where • when • what

got lost

Card 3

who • where • when • what

won a contest

who • where • when • what

broke my arm

How to Write a Story

who • where • when • what

caught a magic fish

How to Write a Story

who • where • when • what

late for school

How to Write a Story

who • where • when • what

buying new shoes

© Evan-Moor Corp. • EMC 799

How to Write a Story

who • where • when • what

lost my lunch money

© Evan-Moor Corp. • EMC 799

How to Write a Story

who • where • when • what

building a doghouse

© Evan-Moor Corp. • EMC 799

How to Write a Story

who • where • when • what

going on a trip

© Evan-Moor Corp. • EMC 799

who • where • when • what

baked cookies

© Evan-Moor Corp. • EMC 799

who • where • when • what

caught a strange animal

© Evan-Moor Corp. • EMC 799

Note: Use the cards on pages 66–70 with "Start with a Picture" on page 44.

Start with a Picture

How to Write a Story

Start with a Picture

How to Write a Story

Start with a Picture

© Evan-Moor Corp. • EMC 799

Start with a Picture

© Evan-Moor Corp. • EMC 799

Start with a Picture

Start with a Picture

Start with a Picture

How to Write a Story

Start with a Picture

How to Write a Story

Story-Writing Centers

Start with a Picture

How to Write a Story

Start with a Picture

How to Write a Story

Story Prompts

I saw a bunny in the garden. It was...

How to Write a Story

Story Prompts

Sam and Pam went to the park...

How to Write a Story

Story Prompts

My puppy was digging a hole. She found a...

How to Write a Story

Story Prompts

Mike was flying his kite. The string broke. His kite...

How to Write a Story

Story Prompts

Kim was late for school. She could not find one of her shoes...

How to Write a Story

Story Prompts

Pete was an old dog. Now his owner had two little kittens...

How to Write a Story

How to Write a Story • EMC 799 • © Evan-Moor Corp.

Carlos was looking for his lost mitt. Instead, he found...

How to Write a Story

We sailed up to the beach. What a pretty island! What will we find when we land?

How to Write a Story

Carmen and her dad went fishing at the lake. When Carmen pulled in her hook and line, she saw...

How to Write a Story

Story Prompts

A hungry rabbit peeked out of his hole. He saw a fox. "How can I get by that fox?" he asked.

How to Write a Story

Story Prompts

"My truck has broken down. What do I do now?" The farmer didn't know that help was already coming his way.

How to Write a Story

Story Prompts

Anna needed money to buy a gift. Mr. Brown hired her to walk his dog. As Anna started up the street with the big dog, …

How to Write a Story

One day, Bear woke up in his cave. The sleepy bear poked his head out and saw...

Pete wanted to win the contest. All he had to do was guess how many jelly beans were in the big jar.

It is always fun to go to my Uncle Mark's farm. This visit we are going to...

Story Prompts

My birthday is next Friday. Mom says I can plan my own party.

How to Write a Story

Story Prompts

I am in big trouble!
I didn't mean to...

How to Write a Story

Story Prompts

Miriam had a strange dream last night. She dreamed that...

How to Write a Story

Note: Use the forms on pages 77–83 with "Story Parts" on page 45.

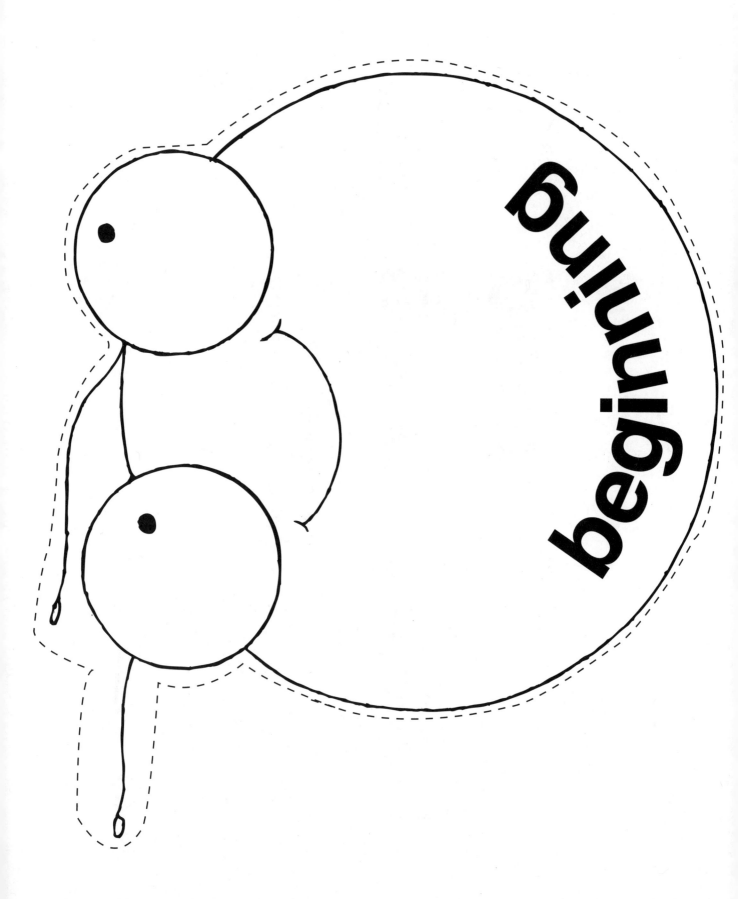

beginning

middle

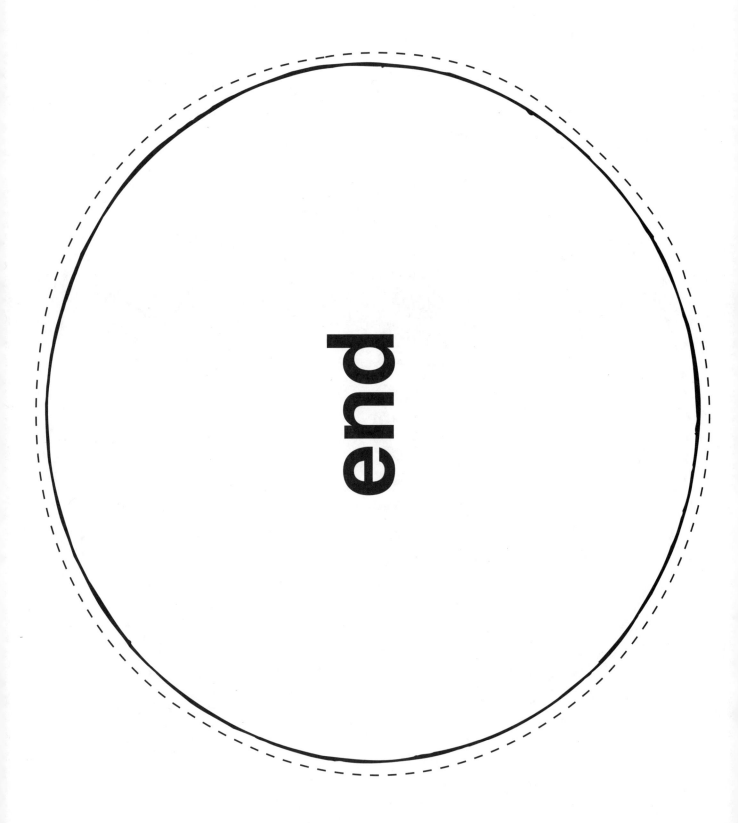

end

Name: _____

Who is the story about?

beginning

_____

_____

_____

_____

_____

_____

_____

_____

_____

_____

_____

Name: _____

What happened?

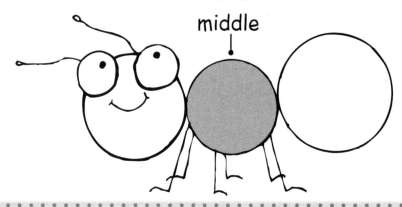

middle

_____

_____

_____

_____

_____

_____

_____

_____

_____

_____

_____

_____

Name: _____

How does the story end?

end

Note: Use the patterns on pages 84–94 for "Train Tales" on page 45.

Write a Story!

Write a Story!

Cut out and glue the engine parts together. Pin the train cars together on the bulletin board.

**Base of Train
Engine Pattern**

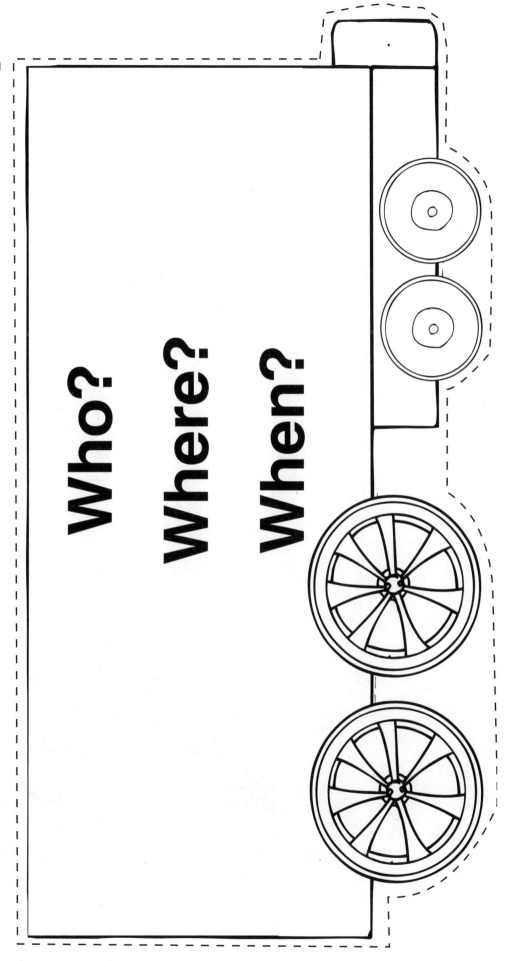

Who?

Where?

When?

Add-on Parts for the Engine

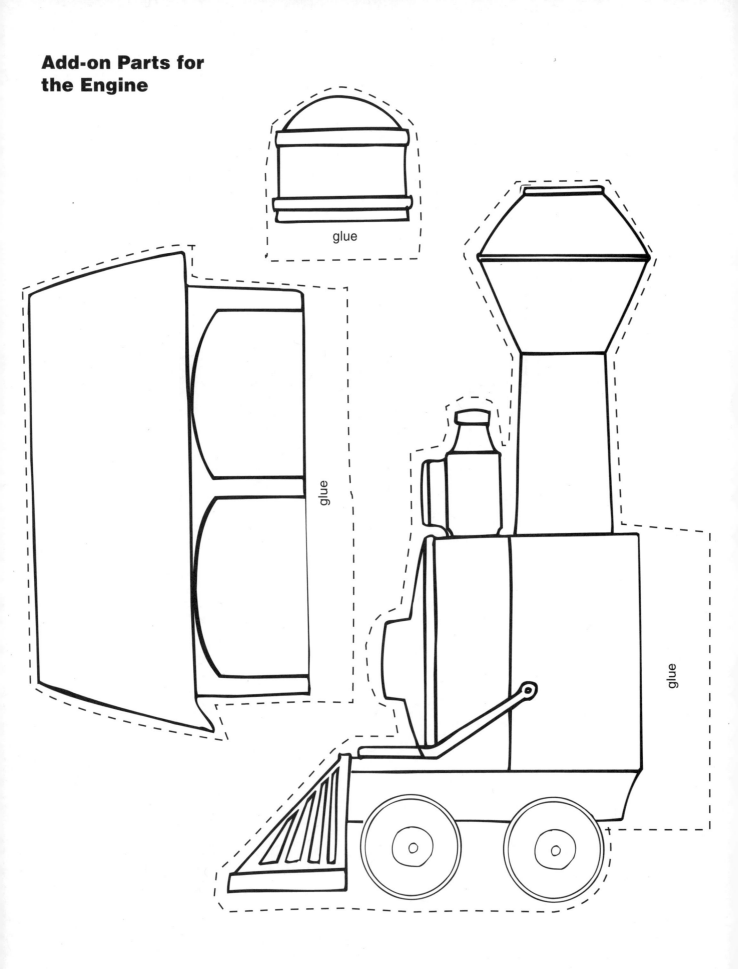

glue

glue

glue

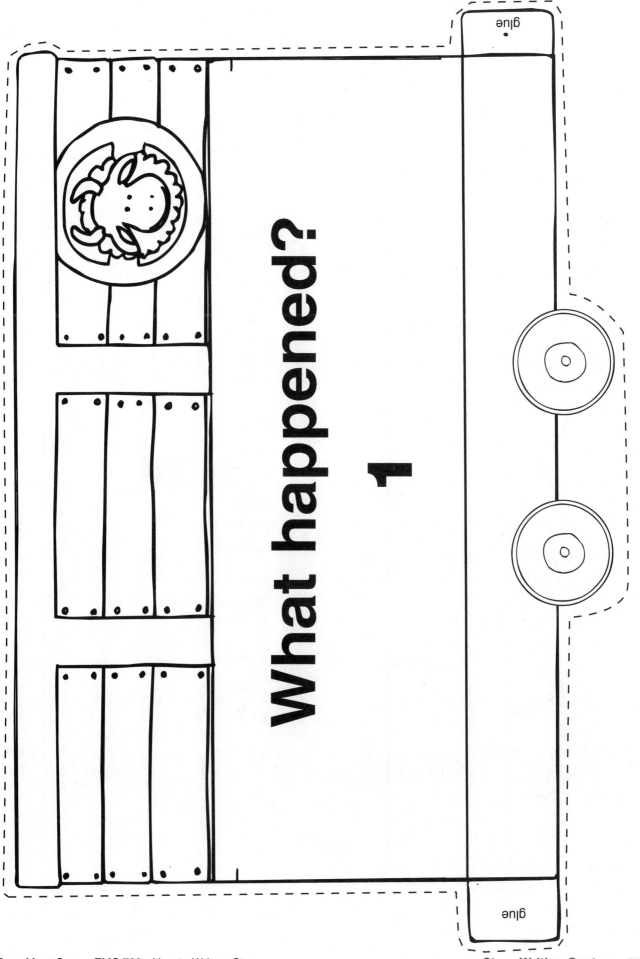

What happened?

1

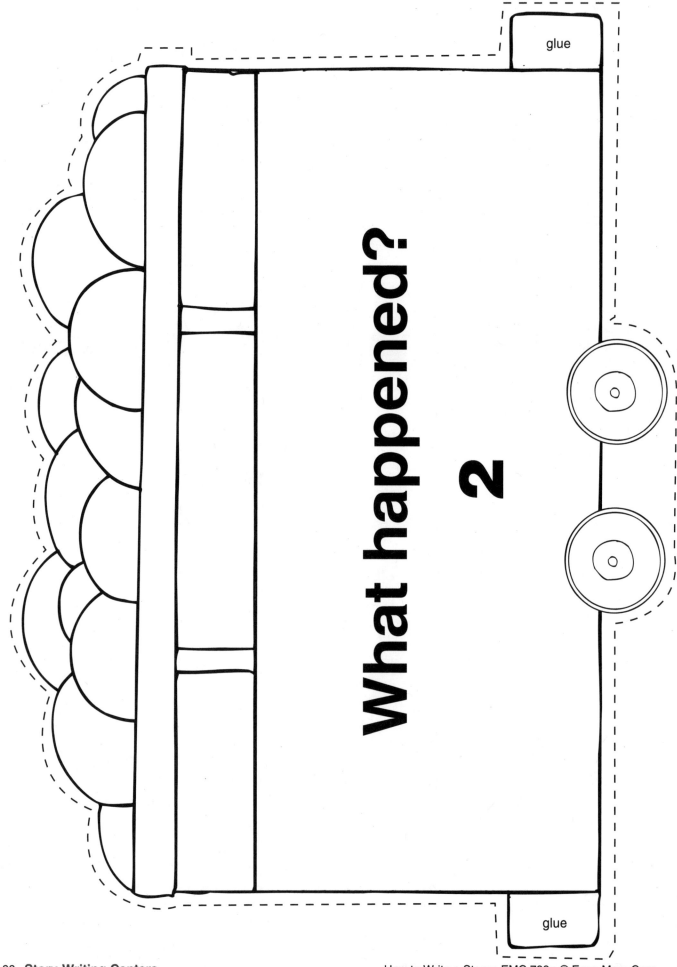

glue

What happened?

2

glue

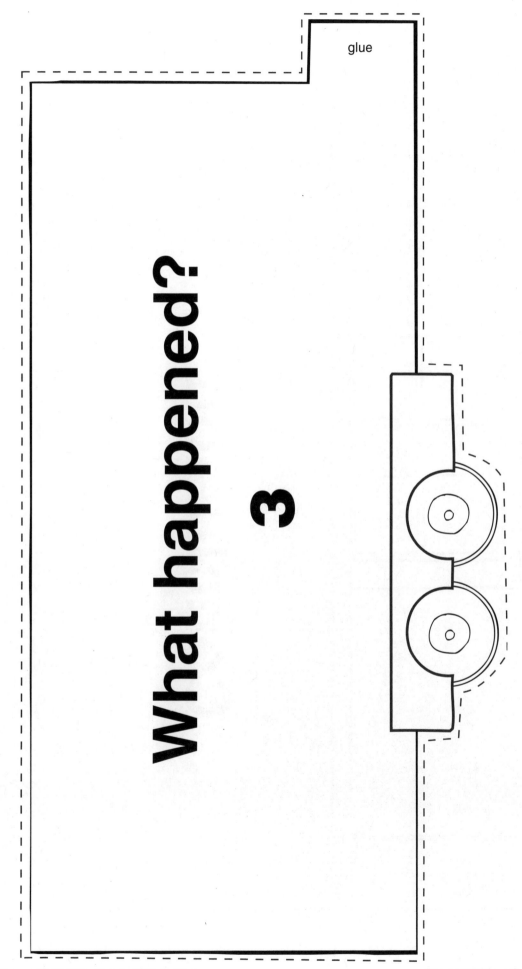

glue

What happened?

3

Story-Writing Centers   89

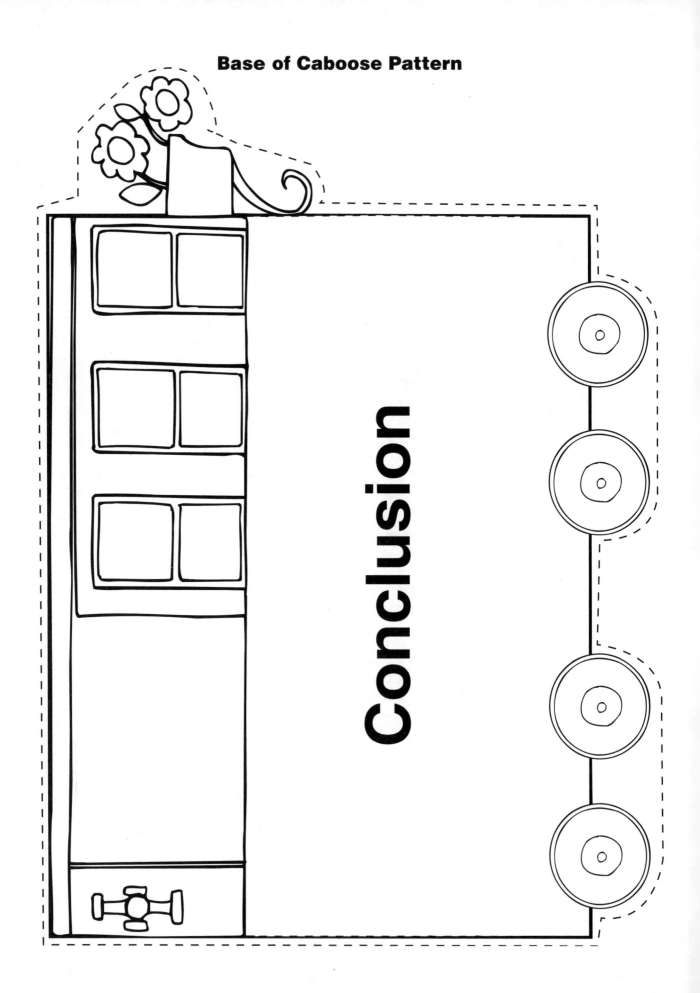

Conclusion

Note: Glue these parts to the caboose pattern as shown.

Caboose

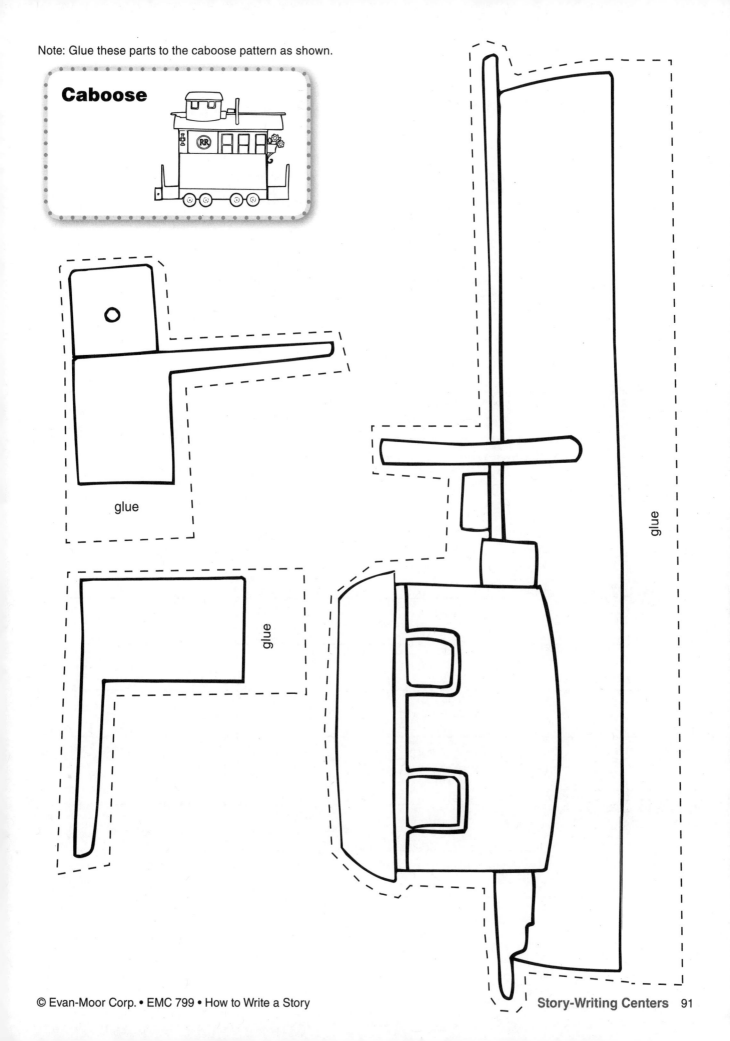

glue

glue

glue

Name: _____

Story Beginning

Who _____

_____

_____

_____

Where _____

_____

_____

_____

When _____

_____

_____

_____

What Happened?

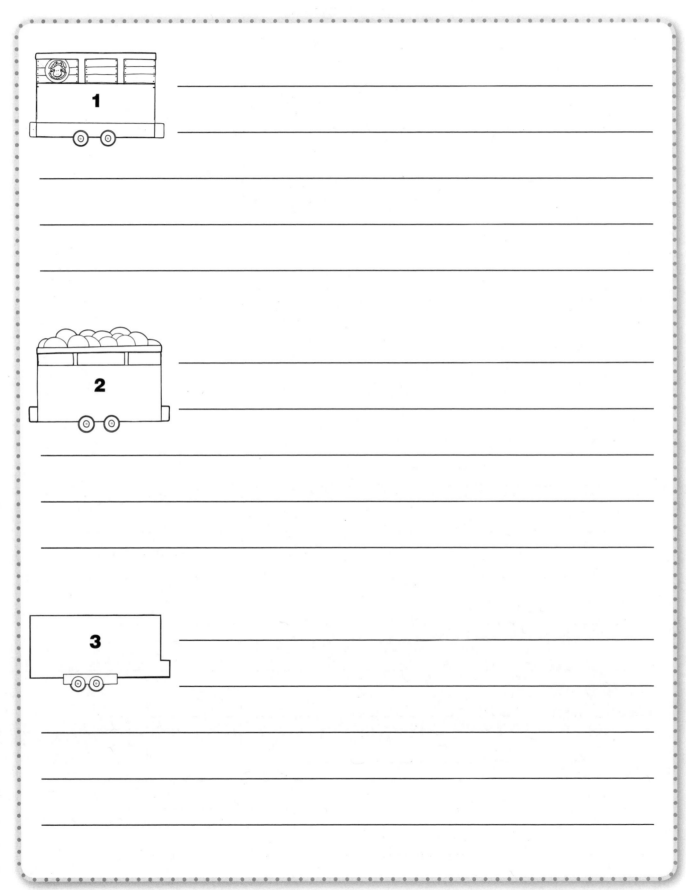

How Does the Story End?

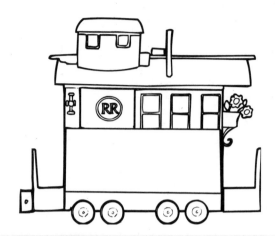

_____

_____

_____

_____

_____

_____

_____

_____

_____

_____

_____

Put Pizzazz in the Publishing Writing Process!

Draw...Then Write

Creative drawing inspires creative writing!

Grades 1–6   The simple drawing steps and fun topics make even the most reluctant of writers excited to write stories. Students follow step-by- step drawing lessons and write about the completed pictures. The reproducible pages are also ideal for writing center activities. 96 pages. Federal funding sources: I, V, 21

www.evan-moor.com/drawwrite

Teacher's Edition Print		Teacher's Edition E-book	
GRADE	EMC	GRADE	EMC
1–3	731-C16	1–3	731i-C16
4–6	773-C16	4–6	773i-C16

The Ultimate Shape Book

Grades K–2   Publish your students' work using delightful book-making forms that cover 50 topics ranging from animals to popular holidays. This comprehensive resource provides a diversity of forms and teaching tips to support the multiple levels of writers in one classroom. Separate forms for emergent, beginning, and independent writers make it easy. 304 pages. Federal funding sources: I, V, 21

www.evan-moor.com/shape

Teacher's Edition Print		Teacher's Edition E-book	
GRADE	EMC	GRADE	EMC
K–2	6000-C16	K–2	6000i-C16

How to Report on Books

Grades PreK–6   Interesting projects to help students explore and report on books, including bookmarks, pop-ups, and puppet forms. 96 pages of time-saving reproducibles and clever ideas! Correlated to state standards. Federal funding sources: I, III, V, ER, RF, 21

www.evan-moor.com/reportbooks

Teacher's Edition Print		Teacher's Edition E-book	
GRADE	EMC	GRADE	EMC
PreK–K	6007-C16	PreK–K	6007i-C16
1–2	6008-C16	1–2	6008i-C16
3–4	6009-C16	3–4	6009i-C16
5–6	6010-C16	5–6	6010i-C16

Take It to Your Seat: Writing Centers

Grades 1–6   Packed with a wide array of writing tips, models, prompts, word banks, and 13 full-color centers! Your students will love the hands-on centers and reproducible practice activities, and you'll love watching their writing skills improve and their portfolios grow! Each title offers interesting, age-appropriate writing topics from poems and postcards to letters and newspaper articles. 192 full-color pages. Correlated to state standards. Federal funding sources: I, V, 21

www.evan-moor.com/twcent

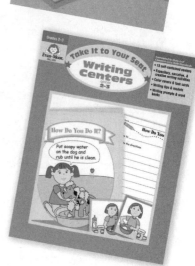

Teacher's Edition Print	
GRADE	EMC
1–2	6002-C16
2–3	6003-C16
3–4	6004-C16
4–5	6005-C16
5–6	6006-C16

Evan-Moor's
9 Best-Selling Writing Titles

How to Write a Story, Grades 1–3
Four step-by-step writing units help young writers create sensible stories with a beginning, a middle, and an end. Includes a story-writing center with reproducible charts, prompts, and writing forms. 96 pages.
Correlated to state standards.
Grades 1–3   EMC 799

How to Write a Story, Grades 4–6
Includes lessons and reproducibles to help students learn the parts of a story, reproducible planning forms, and guidelines for writing in six different genres. Includes a story-writing center with reproducible charts, prompts, and writing forms. 96 pages.
Correlated to state standards.
Grades 4–6   EMC 794

Writing Poetry with Children
A step-by-step guide for teaching students to write couplets, cinquains, haiku, and limericks. Includes reproducible instructions and illustrated writing forms. 96 pages.
Correlated to state standards.
Grades 1–6   EMC 734

Poetry Patterns & Themes
Includes lessons and reproducible forms for 41 types of poetry, including couplets, haiku, limericks, and recipe poetry. 96 pages.
Correlated to state standards.
Grades 3–6   EMC 733

Write a Super Sentence
Through 15 step-by-step guided lessons, students brainstorm adjectives, nouns, verbs, and where-and-when phrases, and use them to expand a simple sentence. Includes reproducible student activity pages and a writing center. 64 pages.
Correlated to state standards.
Grades 1–3   EMC 205

Paragraph Writing
Includes teaching ideas, reproducible forms, and a paragraph-writing center. Topics include parts of a paragraph, types of paragraphs, and planning paragraphs. 80 pages.
Correlated to state standards.
Grades 2–4   EMC 246

Writing Fabulous Sentences & Paragraphs
Lessons and activities progress from writing sentences to writing paragraphs. Complete teacher instructions and over 70 reproducible models and student writing forms. Includes an answer key. 112 pages.
Correlated to state standards.
Grades 4–6   EMC 575

Giant Write Every Day—Daily Writing Prompts
300 "Quickwrites"—25 topics each month for short, daily practice; 202 story starters and titles for longer, more formal writings; 141 reproducible writing forms. 12 monthly sections. 176 pages.
Correlated to state standards.
Grades 2–6   EMC 775

Writing Forms—Tops & Bottoms
Students will be motivated to do their best work when you showcase their reports, stories, or handwriting, by putting their papers in the middle of these two-piece forms. 160 pages.
Grades K–2   EMC 596